- OUTDOOR ADVENTURE GUIDES -

BACKPACKING HACKS

Camping Tips for Outdoor Adventures

by Raymond Bean

Consultant: Gabriel J. Gassman
Outdoor Professional

CAPSTONE PRESS
a capstone imprint

Capstone Captivate is published by Capstone Press, an imprint of Capstone.
1710 Roe Crest Drive
North Mankato, Minnesota 56003
www.capstonepub.com

Copyright © 2020 Capstone. All rights reserved. No part of this publication may be reproduced in whole or in part, or stored in a retrieval system, or transmitted in any form or by any means, electronic, mechanical, photocopying, recording, or otherwise, without written permission of the publisher.

Cataloging-in-Publication Data is available on the Library of Congress website.
ISBN: 978-1-5435-9031-9 (library binding)
ISBN: 978-1-4966-6616-1 (paperback)
ISBN: 978-1-5435-9032-6 (eBook PDF)

Summary: Provides useful tricks and tips for backpacking and camping, including surviving in the wilderness, practicing hygiene, cooking, playing outdoor games, and packing a backpack.

Editorial Credits
Editor: Kellie M. Hultgren; Designer: Juliette Peters;
Media Researcher: Morgan Walters; Production Specialist: Katy LaVigne

Photo Credits
Alamy: Timothy Epp, bottom left 15; Capstone Studio: Karon Dubke, bottom left cover, bottom left 13, top right 15, top right 25, bottom left 25, top right 35; iStockphoto: DonNichols, middle 24, LeoPatrizi, 14, Paigefalk, top 6, PeopleImages, 43; Newscom: Ferrari/ZUMA Press, middle left 17; Shutterstock: Africa Studio, top 9, Alena Ozerova, 32, aliaksei kruhlenia, design element throughout, Anton Foltin, 7, Anton Starikov, top right 21, Blue Planet Studioonkey Business Images, 5, Brian Goodman, top right 33, Chris Comber, bottom left 33, Diego Cervo, bottom 27, Dreamframer, 28, Dzha33, 18, e.backlund, top 13, Elizaveta Galitckaia, bottom right 35, Henrik Larsson, bottom right 34, Iron Mary, top 41, middle 41, bottom 41, Iurii Kachkovskyi, 12, Jerry-Rainey, bottom left 22, johan kusuma, 38, josefkubes, bottom right 33, JudeAnd, 37, Losonsky, top left 34, lukethelake, top left 21, mdbildes, top 24, MintImages, 36, mitzy, middle left 35, Monkey Business Images, 1, 4, MPH Photos, 31, Patiwat Sariya, Cover, Patrick Poendl, 20, photka, bottom left 21, Photo Spirit, top right 17, rawf8, 29, Sean Xu, top 27, Sergey Mironov, 44, Sergiy Kuzmin, bottom right 21, shutter_o, bottom 9, SlayStorm, 8, Steve Collender, (duct tape) design element throughout, TDway, 42, Tim Mainiero, bottom right 22, Tiramisu Studio, bottom 6, Valeev, (moss) design element throughout, VBVVCTND, (khaki) design element throughout, VectorShow, 39, Vishnevskiy Vasily, 30, welcomia, 19, Yuganov Konstantin, 10, ZDL, 23, Zurijeta, 40

All internet sites appearing in back matter were available and accurate when this book was sent to press.

Printed in the United States 5469

TABLE OF CONTENTS

CHAPTER 1
PREPARATION AND PLANNING 4

CHAPTER 2
FOOD, WATER, AND SHELTER 12

CHAPTER 3
KEEPING IT CLEAN 20

CHAPTER 4
CRITTERS AND FIRE 28

CHAPTER 5
HAVE SOME FUN 36

HACK YOUR PACK! 44

GLOSSARY 46
READ MORE 47
INTERNET SITES 47
INDEX 48

Words in **bold** are in the glossary.

CHAPTER 1
PREPARATION AND PLANNING

When people think about outdoor adventures, they often imagine scenes from movies and TV. Hikers get stranded in awful places in bad **weather**. They get cold and wet. They even have to eat bugs to survive! These survival stories are fun to watch, but they aren't common in real life.

Whether you're a seasoned camper or a nervous newbie, you don't have to worry about eating bugs. Smart planning can help make your outdoor adventures safe and enjoyable.

SURVIVING VS. THRIVING IN THE WILD

Will you survive or thrive in the wild? Surviving in the wild means being uncomfortable, hungry, and stressed out. You do whatever it takes to stay alive. Thriving in the wild means being comfortable, well fed, and relaxed. It means enjoying your trip and feeling excited about the next one.

Read on for hacks and tips to help you thrive on your next adventure!

WEATHER WATCHING

Are you going for a quick hike? Or are you taking a weeklong camping trip? Either way, it's not smart to just throw random stuff in your pack. You need a plan.

Learn about the **climate** where you're going. Climate is what the weather is usually like in a place at a certain time of year. What clothing will you need? Will you need rain gear or a warm coat?

In some climates, temperatures are likely to stay the same for most of the day. In other climates, temperatures can change a lot. Some deserts are hot in the daytime and cold at night. In the mountains the weather can change several times in one day. You might experience all four seasons before lunch!

Remember that weather can change suddenly. The climate might usually be warm and dry where you're going. But when you arrive, the weather that day could be cool and wet. Will you be prepared? Make sure you pack for surprises.

COMFORT

Are you the type of person who wears shorts on a snowy day? Or do you wear a winter hat on chilly summer mornings? Knowing yourself will help you hack your pack. Make sure you have what *you* will need to stay comfortable outdoors.

Do you usually want to be warmer or cooler? You can plan for both with one simple hack. Bring two reusable sports bottles and several resealable bags, along with your sleeping bag.

If you're always cold, plan for these heating hacks.

➜ Fill two bottles with warm water. Seal them tight and bring them into your sleeping bag. Hug one like a teddy bear and place another at your feet. The warm water will keep you warm all night.

➜ When you go to sleep, put the next day's clothes in a resealable bag and tuck them into the bottom of your sleeping bag. When you wake in the morning, your clothes will be clean and warm.

➜ When you feel a chill, do some jumping jacks to get your blood pumping and your temperature up.

If you're always hot, the same items will keep you cool.

➤ Use the two water bottles in your sleeping bag, but fill them with cold water.

➤ When you go to sleep, put the next day's clothes in a resealable bag and stick them in your cooler. In the morning, you'll be cooled off right away by your duds.

➤ Wear clothes that are easy to remove, such as snap pants and zipper jackets.

➤ Stay near water. Water tends to be cooler than the land around it.

FACT

The average internal body temperature for a human being is 98.6 degrees Fahrenheit (37 degrees Celsius). But comfort is different for every person. At the same temperature, some people might feel cold while others feel hot.

MAKE A PLAN

Do your homework. Once you know where you will be going, what more can you learn?

DAYTRIP TIPS

Make your daytrip plan at least one day before you go. Study trail maps. Are there things you are excited to see? Circle them on the map so you can find them.

Did you know that you can read reviews of park trails online? You can also look up pictures of your trail before you go.

OVERNIGHT TIPS

Longer trips need more planning. Do you need to reserve a spot at a campsite? What do you need to be comfortable? Pick a good spot on the camp map.

➤ Read camp websites for advice on where to set up.

➤ Pick a spot far away from the camp's garbage area and toilets.

➤ Arriving late or leaving early? Pick a spot where you won't disturb others.

Some campers set up along the trail instead of at a campsite. Can you set up wherever you want? If the trail is busy, pick two or three places where you can camp. That way, if someone has beaten you to the spot, you'll have backup camps.

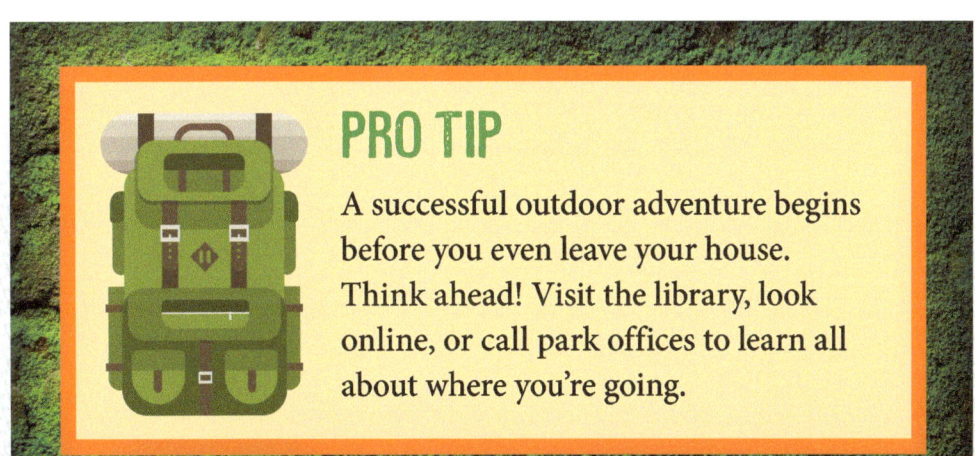

PRO TIP

A successful outdoor adventure begins before you even leave your house. Think ahead! Visit the library, look online, or call park offices to learn all about where you're going.

CHAPTER 2
FOOD, WATER, AND SHELTER

You need three basics for survival: food, water, and shelter. If you plan well, you will survive. But how can you thrive?

EATING WELL

Packing food for an outdoor adventure can be tough. If you bring too much food, it will spoil and go to waste. If you don't bring enough food, *you* will spoil and go to waste! Go beyond the basics with these tips.

PRO TIP

Bring whole fruit for snacks. Fruit is easy to eat on the go. Apples, oranges, and bananas make perfect backpacking snacks. They do not come with plastic wrappers or other waste.

EGGS, ANYONE?

Eggs are a great food for outdoor adventures. They are packed with protein to give you energy. But traveling with eggs can be tricky. So crack 'em to hack 'em! Just before you leave:

1. Crack an egg and scramble it in a cup with a spout.
2. Pour the egg into a clean plastic bottle with the label removed.
3. Use a permanent marker to draw a line on the bottle where the egg ends. Label it 1.
4. Scramble a second egg and pour it into the bottle. Mark the fill level with another line and the number 2.
5. Repeat for as many eggs as you'll need.
6. Store the bottle inside a resealable bag in a cooler.
7. When you're ready to cook, pour out the amount of eggs needed into a hot pan. You will have a hearty meal in no time!

WATCH YOUR WATER

You may be surprised at how much water you'll need on your adventure. Some outdoor places have easy access to drinking water, but others won't.

Before you leave, always make sure you'll have clean drinking water on your adventure. Ask an adult to help. You can read about where you're going online or in a guidebook. When you get there, check the map and remember where to find water. And be sure to bring a reusable bottle or two with you.

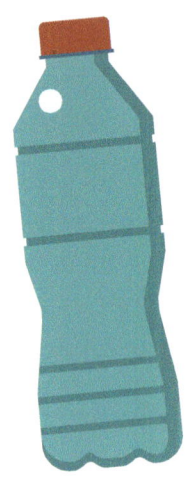

PUT YOUR H₂O TO WORK

Use bottles of frozen water to keep your cooler chilled. A layer of frozen bottles at the bottom of your cooler will keep food from spoiling. As the water melts, you'll have plenty of clean drinking water. And the water stays in the bottles, so your food stays dry.

Turn a tiny light into a bright bottle lantern. Simply attach a headlamp to the bottom of a clear water bottle and turn it on.

JUST IN CASE

Buy a personal water filter or water purification tablets in case of an emergency. These allow you to drink out of streams, rivers, and lakes without worrying about getting sick.

HOME AWAY FROM HOME

Sleeping in a tent can be lumpy, dark, and uncomfortable. With a few handy hacks you can turn a basic tent into a cozy retreat.

GROUND TENTS

- Bring foam floor tiles to line the floor of your tent. They are easy on your feet and keep you warm too.

- Hang solar string lights inside your tent. Charge the solar cell outside your tent during the day for a warm welcome at night.

- Ever tripped on a tent rope? Ow! Avoid injury by marking ropes and poles with pool noodles. Cut a foam noodle into chunks and make a lengthwise slit to hold the rope.

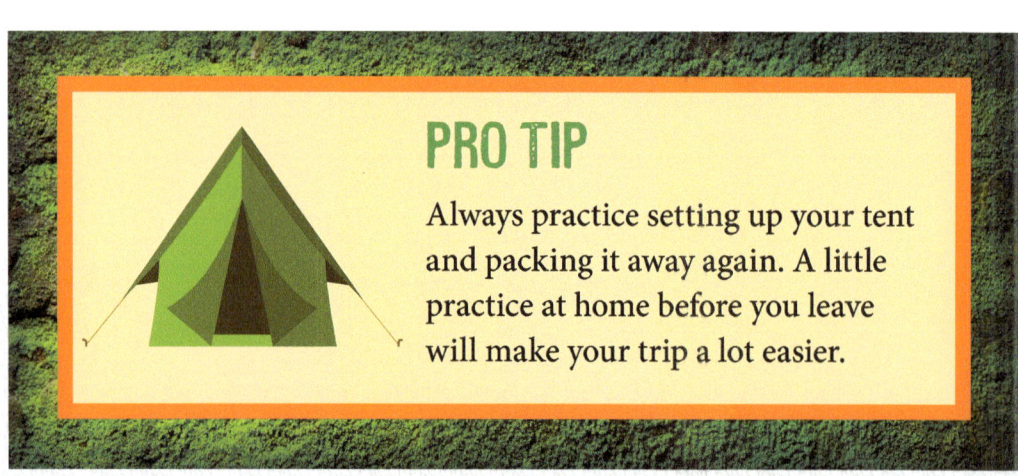

PRO TIP

Always practice setting up your tent and packing it away again. A little practice at home before you leave will make your trip a lot easier.

GET OFF THE GROUND!

Take your camp to the next level! You can get a tiny hanging pod for one person or a large hanging tent for the whole family.

Floating tents are cool, comfy, and super fun! Just be sure that you can't float away while you sleep.

However you get off the ground, check with the park or campground first to make sure it's okay. And always get an adult's help when you set up these tents.

CAMP COMFORT

Camping is fun, but we don't all want to rough it. Use these tips for extra comfort. Don't spend your trip wishing you were home!

Set your tent up on top of a large tarp or ground cloth. This keeps the bottom of the tent dry and helps you stay warmer.

Pillows take up lots of space. Bring a pillowcase instead. Stuff it with your jacket or clean clothes for a comfy pillow.

As the outside temperature changes, the inside of your tent—and your bed—can get damp. To stay dry, roll up your sleeping bag when not using it. Store it in a closed plastic bag to keep water out.

Are rocks and roots keeping you awake? Bring an inflatable mattress or pool float to place under your sleeping bag. It will also help you stay warm.

Bring lots of clean socks and keep them in a sealed bag. You can never have enough dry socks!

Bring an inflatable camp chair for campfire luxury!

PRO TIP

Are cold, wet shoes ruining your comfort after a long day? Dry them out with newspaper. Stuff each shoe full of paper, and the pages will draw the water out overnight.

CHAPTER 3
KEEPING IT CLEAN

Keeping yourself and your camp clean is important on any outdoor adventure. A dirty camp can invite wild animals, insects, and **bacteria** into your space. Human trash can harm wildlife. Aim to have a clean camp, body, and mind in the wild.

WILDERNESS POOPING

Okay, let's just say it. . . . If you're camping, sooner or later you're going to have to go to the bathroom. Most campsites have bathrooms and even showers. But if you're out on the trail when nature calls, you need to be prepared.

WHAT YOU'LL NEED

In many wilderness areas, you are not allowed to leave any trash behind. Whatever you bring in, you must take it out . . . even if it's gross. So bring a small "poopin' pack" with these items:

One bag is for clean supplies and the other is for dirty toilet paper and wipes. After you go, put the used toilet paper and wipes in the dirty bag and wipe your hands with sanitizer. When you reach a garbage can, throw out your dirty bag.

CAT HOLE

What is a cat hole? It's a hole in the ground that you poop in. If you'll be camping far from any toilets, bring your poopin' pack and a small **trowel** or folding camp shovel.

The number-one thing about making number two is to always do it at least 200 feet (61 meters) from your campsite. Make sure the area is not in use by others. Stay away from your water sources too.

PRO TIP

If you don't have toilet paper, you can use leaves and then bury them in the cat hole. But be sure you know which leaves to avoid! Poison ivy and poison oak can cause an itchy rash. If you're not sure if the leaf is safe, leave it alone.

POISON OAK

POISON IVY

1. Find several places that are free of roots and rocks so you can dig easily.

2. Use your trowel or shovel to dig a hole 6 to 8 inches (15 to 20 centimeters) deep and 4 to 6 inches (10 to 15 cm) across in each place.

3. Mark each cat hole with a stick or other marker so you can find it in a hurry or in the dark. Lay the marker across the filled hole after doing your thing. This signals other campers not to use the same spot.

4. When you use the cat hole, don't leave toilet paper or wipes behind. Animals might dig them up and make a mess.

CLEAN BODY

If you spend more than a day or two in the wild, you will need to bathe. Nobody likes a stinky hiker!

Forget carrying a whole bar of wet, slippery soap. Before you leave, carefully cut a bar of **biodegradable** soap into thin slices or small cubes. Place them in a resealable bag. Use one at a time for a quick wash in a lake, stream, or hanging shower.

Keep germs and dirt off your toothbrush. Bring a toothbrush case or a plastic cap for the brush end.

PRO TIP

Ask a park ranger whether it's okay to bathe in streams and lakes. In some places it's not safe to get in the water. And some kinds of soap can be harmful to wildlife.

Toothpaste tubes can easily pop in your pack. Try this hack instead.

1. A week before you leave, squeeze out small dots of toothpaste onto a piece of aluminum foil.
2. Make at least two dots for each day you'll be on the trail.
3. Allow the dots to dry for three or four days.
4. Peel the dots off the foil and place them in a resealable bag or small plastic container. Add a small amount of baking powder and shake to keep them from sticking together.

5. When it's time to brush on the trail, simply pop one dot in your mouth, chew, and brush like you usually would at home.
6. Don't spit all of your toothpaste out in the same place. It could attract animals. Spread it out over a large area. Or spit in a clean cat hole and cover it up.

CLEAN MIND

You're in nature! Take time to quiet down and enjoy the beauty around you. When you get quiet, you'll connect to the natural world in a new way.

1. Find a safe, quiet place.
2. Sit in a comfortable position.
3. Straighten your back.
4. Keep your head up. (Don't fall asleep!)
5. Close your eyes.
6. Breathe in and out in long, slow breaths.
7. Don't think. Just listen.
8. Pay attention to your senses. What do you hear and smell?
9. Keep breathing until you feel completely relaxed. Just five minutes of quiet time in nature can make you feel great!

FOREST BATHING

In Japan many people practice shinrin-yoku. This translates to "forest bathing." It is a way to increase health. Spending time with trees can put you in a good mood and help you feel less stressed. It can even help you sleep better.

CHAPTER 4
CRITTERS AND FIRE

You already know that you should not leave food out in your camp. It's common sense. But what else can you do to make sure unwanted critters and pests leave you alone in the wild?

INSECTS

Store-bought insect sprays keep all kinds of bugs away. If you don't like harsh chemicals, try some of these tips instead.

Put dryer sheets in your sleeping bag, your shoes, your pack, your cooler, and anywhere else you want to stay critter-free. Many bugs dislike the smell.

PRO TIP

Some smells that bugs dislike can attract bears and other animal visitors. If you are camping near wild animals, wear long sleeves and pants to keep bugs away from you instead.

Go natural. The smell of sage, lavender, **citronella**, cedar, and other oils **repels** pests.

Spray a mix of water and peppermint oil to keep ants away from your food.

Citronella oil and tea tree oil help keep mosquitos away. Spray or dab some on your wrists, ankles, neck, and forehead.

Geranium oil on your ankles and socks helps repel ticks and horseflies. Tuck your pant cuffs into the tops of your socks for extra protection.

Burning the herbs sage and rosemary in your campfire helps keep several kinds of insects away.

ANIMALS

Wildlife watching is fun . . . but not when animals steal your breakfast! Don't leave food out where animals might be tempted to pay you a visit. Hungry animals can damage camps and even hurt campers. And human food can make wild animals sick. Keep food stored and sealed when you're not eating.

Some foods can send animals away from your tent. The strong smells of garlic, vinegar, cloves, and spicy cayenne pepper can drive mice and raccoons away. But beware! Strong cooking smells will attract bears to your camp. If you're camping in bear country, don't use food to repel pests.

PRO TIP

If you will be camping in or near bear territory, pack bear spray. Be sure to read the directions on the can before you leave.

FIRE

Fire starting is an important wilderness skill. You never know when you'll need to stay warm in a tough situation. But most of the time, you just want a cheery fire to cook dinner or toast marshmallows.

FIRE SAFETY

Never start a fire without an adult's help. Fires can spread quickly and endanger people, animals, and habitats. Check with a park ranger to make sure fires are okay. Responsible campers have a healthy respect for fire and fire safety.

FIRE-STARTING HACKS

Matches are the easiest way to start a fire. Keep them dry in a waterproof bag or box.

Learn to use a flint and steel. When you scrape the steel against the flint stick, it makes sparks. It can be used over and over again, even after it gets wet.

If you have trouble turning sparks into flame, try these hacks.

Bring a resealable bag of **tinder**, such as dryer lint, cotton balls, or wood shavings. These materials are easy to set on fire with matches or sparks.

Pine sap is highly flammable. Collect some from a pine sap bubble. Rub it on small sticks and leaves and add them to your tinder.

Many delicious snack chips make great tinder. They are made with oil, which is highly flammable. Experiment with your favorite chips before you go. If you don't need them for fire, you will still have a tasty snack!

Bring birthday candles to help you get a fire going in a pinch. They burn longer than matches.

Hand sanitizer contains alcohol, which is flammable. Spray some on your tinder and you will have a fire in no time.

CHAPTER 5
HAVE SOME FUN

Every outdoor adventure is full of surprises. But if it rains, you'll want to make some fun of your own. Plan ahead to stay busy and not bored.

CRAFTS AND GAMES

Nature is a great place to play. You can make art with what you find in the wild. And you can play games without a board or computer. As you explore, just look around you for ideas!

ROCK OUT

You worked hard to plan this trip. Now make some memories that rock!

WHAT YOU NEED

- Permanent markers or paint pens in a resealable bag
- A few unique rocks that catch your eye during the day

WHAT TO DO

1. Choose one or two rocks that you like. Rocks with smooth surfaces work best.
2. Use the pens to decorate your rocks with fun designs or words. For example, write a word or short phrase that will remind you of the trip.
3. Let the paint dry. (This may take several hours on damp days.)
4. Return any rocks you didn't use to the wild.

PRO TIP

Before moving or painting rocks, check with the park ranger to make sure collecting rocks is permitted.

ROCK BALANCING

People have been stacking stones since ancient times. Make your own stack!

1. Collect a bunch of rocks of different sizes. Flat rocks stack best.
2. See who can stack them highest.
3. When you are done with the game, return the stones to where you found them.

CAMPSITE ALPHABET HUNT

Play I Spy in camp! Take turns naming items related to your adventure. Each person must name an object starting with the next letter in the alphabet.

For example, player one says, "A for aluminum can." Player two says, "B for bags." Player three says, "C for candle," and so on. Keep going until players can't name any more items.

38

SHADOW PUPPETS

Set up a lantern or flashlight so it shines on the side of a tent, large rock, or other surface. Move your hands around to make different-shaped shadows. Experiment with the examples below or invent your own. If you get really good at it, make up a fun story and act it out puppet style.

STARGAZING

The night sky comes alive in the wild. After a busy day, lie back on a chair or on the ground and gaze up at the sky. Bring along a stargazing map and work with your fellow campers to locate as many **constellations** as you can.

See if you can locate these constellations.

Made up of seven stars, Ursa Major, or the Big Dipper, is one of the most famous constellations. Its name is Latin for "greater bear." Look north to find the Big Dipper in the summer.

Ursa Minor is also called the Little Dipper. If you draw a line between the two stars on the front of the Big Dipper's cup, from bottom to top, it will point you to the bright North Star. The North Star marks the end of the Little Dipper's handle.

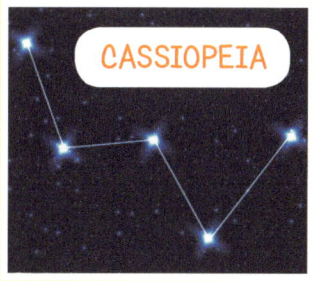

Start where the handle meets the cup of the Big Dipper. Draw a line from there through the North Star. That line points to Cassiopeia, a constellation shaped like a big letter *W* or *M*.

PRO TIP

If you have a smartphone with you, use a star-finder app to help locate stars and constellations.

HAPPY PACK HACKING!

Outdoor adventures are wonderful fun if you make a good plan. Hacking your pack helps you think about what you really need, bring the correct supplies, and learn to go with the flow. Smart tips can make an okay trip into an amazing trip. Now you're ready to thrive in the wild!

PRO TIP

Test your gear. Do a short day hike to check how your backpack fits. Is it comfortable? How much food and water do you need? Use that information to plan longer hikes.

HACK YOUR PACK!

Have a plan when you're packing for your adventure. If you pack with purpose, you'll know where everything is and won't leave anything behind. Here's a suggested packing method.

1. Make a list of everything you plan to bring.
2. Start packing a few days before you leave.
3. Think carefully about everything you plan to bring. Decide if it should go on the bottom, in the middle, up top, or in a pocket.
4. Place the soft, lightweight items you won't need while hiking on the bottom of your pack.
5. Place heavier and odd-shaped items in the middle. Surround them with clothing and other soft items. Fill every nook and cranny of your pack. You don't want items shifting when you move.
6. Put items you need on the trail in the top and outer pockets of your pack.

OUTER POCKETS OF PACK
Things to grab quickly on the trail:

- ❏ bear spray
- ❏ bug spray
- ❏ compass
- ❏ extra batteries
- ❏ headlamp (or flashlight)
- ❏ map
- ❏ multitool
- ❏ phone or camera with waterproof pouch
- ❏ snacks (apple, energy bar, granola bars)
- ❏ sunglasses
- ❏ sunscreen
- ❏ water bottles

TOP OF PACK
Things to reach easily on the trail:

- ❏ fire-starting kit
- ❏ first aid kit
- ❏ lunch
- ❏ rain gear
- ❏ toilet kit
- ❏ travel field guide
- ❏ water filter or purifying tablets

MIDDLE OF PACK
Heavy things for use in camp:

- ❏ camp dishes
- ❏ camp stove and fuel
- ❏ clothing (packed around other items to use all space)
- ❏ 3 or 4 one-gallon resealable bags (fill one with socks)
- ❏ toiletries (soap, toothpaste and toothbrush, comb)
- ❏ entertainment kit (optional):
  roll of string
  bag of markers/paint pens
  small notebook and pencils
  playing cards
  stargazing guide (small)

BOTTOM OF PACK
Lightweight items for use in camp:

- ❏ clothing (packed around other items to use all space)
- ❏ dryer sheets
- ❏ ground tarp
- ❏ jacket
- ❏ pillowcase
- ❏ sleeping bag
- ❏ tent (poles may be tied to side of pack)
- ❏ inflatable sleeping pad (optional)

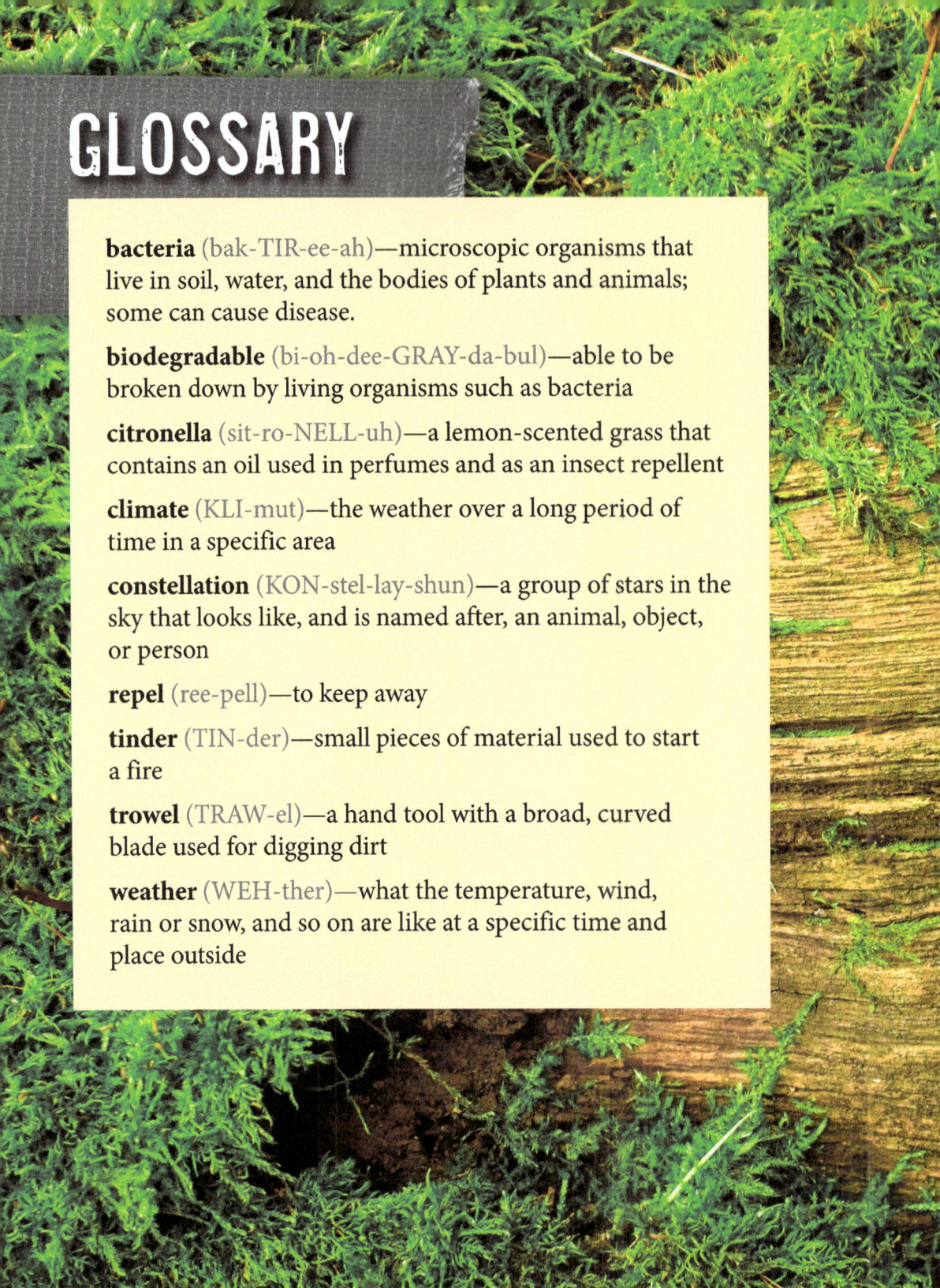

GLOSSARY

bacteria (bak-TIR-ee-ah)—microscopic organisms that live in soil, water, and the bodies of plants and animals; some can cause disease.

biodegradable (bi-oh-dee-GRAY-da-bul)—able to be broken down by living organisms such as bacteria

citronella (sit-ro-NELL-uh)—a lemon-scented grass that contains an oil used in perfumes and as an insect repellent

climate (KLI-mut)—the weather over a long period of time in a specific area

constellation (KON-stel-lay-shun)—a group of stars in the sky that looks like, and is named after, an animal, object, or person

repel (ree-pell)—to keep away

tinder (TIN-der)—small pieces of material used to start a fire

trowel (TRAW-el)—a hand tool with a broad, curved blade used for digging dirt

weather (WEH-ther)—what the temperature, wind, rain or snow, and so on are like at a specific time and place outside

READ MORE

Colson, Rob. *Ultimate Survival Guide for Kids*. Richmond Hill, ON: Firefly Books, 2015.

Miles, Justin. *Ultimate Explorer Guide for Kids*. Richmond Hills, ON: Firefly Books, 2015.

Rey, H. A. *Find the Constellations*. Boston, MA: HMH Books for Young Readers, 2016.

Ward, Alexa. *America's National Parks*. Oakland, CA: Lonely Planet Kids, 2019.

INTERNET SITES

National Park Service: Kids in Parks
https://www.nps.gov/kids/

Star Charts and More
https://in-the-sky.org/

Trail Information at the Hiking Project
https://www.hikingproject.com/

INDEX

animals, 20, 23, 25, 28, 30–31, 32

bathing, 24
bears, 28, 31

campsites, 11, 20, 22
cat holes, 22–23, 25
climate, 6–7
clothes, 8, 9, 18, 19
coolers, 9, 13, 15, 28
cooling, 9
crafts, 37, 38

dampness, 18, 19

eggs, 13

fire, 29, 32–35
flint and steel, 33
floating tents, 17
food, 12–13, 15, 29, 30–31, 35, 43
forest bathing, 26
fruit, 12

games, 38
ground tents, 16

hanging tents, 17
heating, 8

insects, 28–29
I Spy game, 38

maps, 10, 11, 14, 40
matches, 33, 34

packing, 43, 44–45
planning, 6, 10–11, 43, 44
pooping, 20–23
practice, 16, 43

quiet time, 26

rangers, 24, 32, 37
research, 10–11, 14
rock crafts, 37, 38

safety, 15, 22, 24, 30, 32
shadow puppets, 39
shoes, 19, 28
soap, 24, 31
stargazing, 40–41

temperature, 7, 8–9, 18
tents, 16–19
tinder, 34, 35
toothbrushes, 24
toothpaste, 25
trails, 10, 11
trash, 21

water, 8, 9, 14–15, 43
water filters, 15
water purification tablets, 15
weather, 6–7
websites, 10, 11, 14